A Kid's Guide to Salvation

B

ISBN 978-1-963457-02-5

Have you ever wondered how we got here or what the point of everything is? Do you ever wonder why you exist or even why the world exists? Do you ever think about God?

Maybe you believe in God and are looking for more information about what your relationship with Him should look like. Then again, maybe you are not so sure about God, but you are interested in learning more about Him.

Maybe you don't believe in God at all, but you have a parent or grandparent or a friend that does, and you are curious about what they believe.

If any of these describe your situation, then this is the book for you. Hopefully, by the time you read through it and answer the questions that are included, you will understand more about faith and salvation.

Salvation

Salvation is a big word with a big meaning. Some similar words you may have heard before are redemption and deliverance. Salvation means you are saved from something.

Think for a minute and write down some things you could be saved from.

_____

_____

_____

_____

Did you say you could be saved from an accident or a fire? Or maybe drowning? Have you ever been saved from something?

I was once saved from drowning. When I was a kid, my family was at the lake, and I was out in the water floating on a beach ball. I went a little too far in the wrong direction, let go of the ball, and expected to stand up and walk to the shore. But my feet didn't touch the bottom. The water was way too deep. I went underwater and back up again. I swallowed a bunch of water when I tried to yell for help, then went back under again.

Thankfully, my dad saw me struggling and heard my yells. He jumped in the water, grabbed me, and brought me to shore. He saved me.

Being saved means we are protected from harm or even death.

When we talk about salvation, we mean we are saved from something, but not like fire or drowning.

Some would say we need to be saved from the devil. Or money. Others would say we need to be saved from ourselves.

The Bible says we need to be saved from our sins.

Webster's Dictionary tells us salvation means "deliverance from the power and effects of sin."

For that to make sense, we need to understand what sin is. The rest of this book is divided into different sections to help you understand sin:

- What is sin?
- Why do we need to be saved from our sin?
- What is the cost of sin?
- Where did sin come from?
- What was the first sin?
- More!

There may be words in this book you haven't heard before, but hopefully, you will understand as you read and answer questions. If there is something you don't understand, ask your parents or other trusted adult for help.

There will be lots of Bible verses listed, so it will be a good idea to have a Bible with you to look them up as you read. There will also be questions for you to answer to see if you understand.

Faith

Before we get to sin, it is important to understand what faith is.

Have you heard of faith before?

Faith means believing in something you can't see. Look out a window. Can you see the wind? Wind itself is invisible, but you can see the effects of the wind. Wind causes trees to sway; wind causes water in lakes and ponds to move and create waves. Wind blows leaves across the yard and tumbleweeds across the desert. There are many effects of wind that you can see. But you can't see wind itself.

Just because you can't see it doesn't mean it isn't there or doesn't exist. But, it does take faith to believe wind exists. To help you have faith, you look for evidence to support your belief that the wind exists.

Believing in God is similar. We can't see Him, but we can build our faith that He exists by looking for evidence.

We can look to the Bible, which is a historical document that contains records of things that God did throughout history.

We can look to other people. Many times, God will help a person change their actions and attitudes in a way that doesn't seem possible. A changed life is evidence of God working.

We can look at creation itself. Living things are so complex, it actually takes more faith to believe living things evolved from nothing than to believe God created the universe.

This book is not an attempt to prove to you that God exists. There is evidence all around us that God exists, but no one can confidently prove that God exists. That is why it takes faith to believe He exists.

Did you know your faith can grow?

When following Jesus, it doesn't take much faith to believe. When Jesus was on earth, he taught and traveled with a small group of people called disciples. These were people who personally saw Jesus perform miracles. They could see him, hear him, and touch him. But, at times, even they lacked faith.

Luke 17:5 "The apostles said to the Lord, "increase our faith!"

If you only have a little faith or are struggling to believe God is real, I challenge you to begin asking God if He is real, and like the disciples, ask Him to increase your faith.

Do you believe in God?

_____

_____

_____

How would you describe faith?

_____

_____

_____

_____

_____

_____

How can you grow your faith?

_____

_____

_____

_____

_____

I will walk by faith

EVEN WHEN I CANNOT SEE

2 CORINTHIANS 5:7

Sin - what is it?

Read 1 John 3:4-5

Everyone who sins breaks the law; in fact, sin is lawlessness. But you know that he appeared so that he might take away our sins. And in him is no sin.

According to this verse, what is sin?

_____

_____

What do you think that means?

_____

_____

_____

Much of the New Testament was originally written in Greek, and it is sometimes helpful to look at Greek words to help us understand. The most common word for sin in Greek is "hamartanō." The basic idea of hamartano is 'to miss the mark' or 'to fall short'. When combining sin (harmartano) with the law, it means to fall short of living up to what the law says. If we deviate from the law, it is sin.

Let's try something. If you have a Nerf gun, go get it now. If not, grab a ball. If you don't have either, then you can use a pair of socks.

Set up some kind of 'target' across the room. You could use a paper cup, a stuffed animal, a small pillow, or even a shoe. Once you set up the target, back away until you are on the other side of the room. Take careful aim, shoot a dart, or throw the ball (or your socks) and try to hit the target. Did you hit it? If so, try again. If you keep hitting the target, find a smaller target. Keep going until you miss the mark.

Just like you missed the target, there will be times you miss the mark when considering the law. You may be able to hit the target often, but no one is perfect, and eventually, everyone misses the mark with some aspect of the law. In other words, we all fall short. We all sin. We will talk about this more later.

Sin is anything against God's law. But what is the law?

What are some things you can think of that are against the law?

_____

_____

_____

_____

_____

_____

_____

_____

In the Bible, when the law is mentioned there are two main meanings for it. The first is the Law of Moses, otherwise known as the Ten Commandments. God gave Moses a set of stone tablets with the Ten Commandments written on them. They were to be used to guide the lives of the Israelites (and us).

1. You shall have no other gods before Me.
2. You shall make no idols.
3. You shall not take the name of the Lord your God in vain.
4. Keep the Sabbath day holy.
5. Honor your father and your mother.
6. You shall not murder.
7. You shall not commit adultery.
8. You shall not steal.
9. You shall not bear false witness against your neighbor.
10. You shall not covet

The second meaning of Law comes from Jesus himself. When Jesus was asked about the greatest commandment in the law as stated in Matthew 22:36-40

Jesus replied: "'Love the Lord your God with all your heart and with all your soul and with all your mind.' This is the first and greatest commandment. And the second is like it: 'Love your neighbor as yourself.' All the Law and the Prophets hang on these two commandments."

Jesus basically summarized the entire Law with these two statements.

First, we are to love God. Second, we are to love our neighbor. All the Ten Commandments can fit into one of these two categories. Everything God would want from us comes from one of these two commandments.

When the Bible says that sin is lawlessness, that means anything contrary to the law, or these two commandments, is sin. That could be in our actions (or inactions), our speech, or even our thoughts.

In your own words, how would you define sin?

_____

_____

_____

_____

_____

What are some sins you can name?

_____

_____

_____

_____

_____

(In case you need some help, here are some additional examples of sin: lying, cheating, stealing, disobeying, being disrespectful.)

The Ten Commandments

1. PUT GOD FIRST

2. HAVE NO IDOLS

3. RESPECT THE NAME OF GOD

4. REMEMBER THE SABBATH DAY, TO KEEP IT HOLY

5. HONOUR YOUR FATHER AND YOUR MOTHER

6. DO NOT MURDER

7. be faithful in marriage

8. DO NOT STEAL

9. DO NOT LIE

10. DO NOT ENVY WHAT OTHERS HAVE

Have you broken any of the Ten Commandments recently?

_____

_____

_____

_____

When you break one of the Ten Commandments, or knowingly commit any sin, how do you feel?

_____

_____

_____

Can you think of a time you apologized to someone because of a sin?

_____

_____

_____

_____

Where did sin come from?

When God created Adam, He told him he could eat from any tree in the garden, except from the tree of the knowledge of good and evil.

The Lord God took the man and put him in the Garden of Eden to work it and take care of it. And the Lord God commanded the man, "You are free to eat from any tree in the garden; but you must not eat from the tree of the knowledge of good and evil, for when you eat from it you will certainly die." (Genesis 2:15-17)

Remember the definition of sin? Lawlessness? Well, God's command to not eat from the tree of the knowledge of good and evil was the 'law'. And the penalty of that sin was 'death'.

Well guess what? Adam and Eve chose to disobey God and eat the fruit. The devil disguised himself as a serpent and convinced them with lies. Adam and Eve committed the first sin.

Payment for Sin

Now that we know what sin is, it is important to know there is a consequence for sin.

Romans 6:23 for the wages of sin is death

If we have committed sin, our punishment is death. That doesn't mean that we will immediately die if we tell a lie or steal something. What it means is that unforgiven sin will cause our spiritual death.

God's desire for us is that we be forgiven of our sin and live an eternal life with Him. But sin in our life makes that impossible. The alternative to living in Heaven with God forever is living forever separated from God in Hell.

Heaven and Hell are very real places. One was created as an eternal paradise with God, the other as an eternal punishment without God.

The good news is that God has a plan to save us from our sin, and it started way back in the Old Testament.

John 3:16 For God so loved the world that he gave his one and only Son, that whoever believes in him shall not perish but have eternal life.

Adam and Eve sinned when they ate from the tree that God told them to leave alone. After they sinned, they hid. When God came and talked to them, what did He do? He killed an animal and made clothes for them. Their sin was covered through an animal sacrifice.

Later God established a plan with the Israelites and explained that their sin could be covered through a sacrifice of an animal. This was called atonement. Atonement means reparation for an offense or reconciliation of God and man. Atonement was a form of forgiveness of our sin.

Once a year during the Feast of Atonement, people would bring an animal to the temple. The priest would prepare the animal and kill it as a way to cover the sins of the people.

In your own words, what is atonement?

_____

_____

_____

_____

What is the payment for sin?

_____

_____

_____

Hebrews 9:22

22 In fact, the law requires that nearly everything be cleansed with blood, and without the shedding of blood there is no forgiveness.

Leviticus 16:30-34 because on this day atonement will be made for you, to cleanse you. Then, before the LORD, you will be clean from all your sins. It is a day of sabbath rest, and you must deny yourselves; it is a lasting ordinance. The priest who is anointed and ordained to succeed his father as high priest is to make atonement. He is to put on the sacred linen garments and make atonement for the Most Holy Place, for the tent of meeting and the altar, and for the priests and all the members of the community. "This is to be a lasting ordinance for you: Atonement is to be made once a year for all the sins of the Israelites."

The consequence of sin is death. If we don't care and continue living the way we want to with an unrepentant heart and unforgiven sin, we will pay the price of our sin ourselves. That means we will spend an eternity in Hell away from God.

Before Jesus died, God provided a way to atone for sin through a sacrifice (death of an animal). The consequence of sin was still death, but it wasn't the death of a person, it was the death of an animal.

When Jesus came to earth, he became the ultimate sacrifice for our sin, and he died for us.
His death became payment for our sin.

Take a few minutes and answer these questions.

What are consequences?

_____

_____

_____

_____

In your own words, how did the first sin happen?

_____

_____

_____

_____

How were people forgiven of their sin in the Old Testament?

_____

_____

_____

_____

Who is considered a sinner?

_____

_____

_____

Am I a sinner?

_____

_____

_____

What are some things I have done that would be considered sin?

_____

_____

_____

What is the consequence of sin?

_____

_____

_____

All have sinned

Romans 3:23 For all have sinned and fall short of the glory of God

The Bible is clear that ALL have sinned. It doesn't matter how good of a person you are. Being good doesn't keep you from being a sinner. Since Adam and Eve committed the first sin, ALL people have a sinful nature. That means no matter how hard we try, we cannot live a life free of sin.

In fact, in all of history, there was only one person who lived a sinless life.

Who is the only person to never sin?

_____

_____

_____

Christ died for our sin

God's plan for our forgiveness began with animal sacrifices in the Old Testament and included Jesus' death on the cross in the New Testament.

Jesus was sinless and was perfect. He was the perfect spotless lamb and became the only sacrifice necessary for our forgiveness. Once, cleansing of sin was achieved through the sacrifice of an animal, but that was a temporary action and one that needed to be repeated every year. Every year, during the Feast of Atonement, a sacrifice had to be made.

Jesus' death took the place of all sacrifices. Being perfect and sinless, His death meant that an annual sacrifice would no longer be necessary.

The wages, or payment for sin is death. And Jesus paid that debt with His death on the cross. That is why we don't need to make a sacrifice today in order to be forgiven of our sins.

Romans 5:8 While we were still sinners, Christ died for us

John 3:16 For God so loved the world that he gave his one and only Son, that whoever believes in him shall not perish but have eternal life.

God doesn't want you stuck in your sin. God wants you to be forgiven of your sin because He loves you. In fact, He loves you so much that He sent His son Jesus to die for you. Jesus became the ultimate sacrifice for our sin, so we no longer have to regularly atone for our sin like the people in the Old Testament did. Jesus died as a final sacrifice for our sin, so we can be forgiven.

Jesus ♥
LOVES ME

What does perish mean?

_____

_____

_____

_____

Why did Jesus die for us?

_____

_____

_____

_____

Why isn't an animal sacrifice necessary for forgiveness anymore?

_____

_____

_____

_____

Everyone who calls on the name of the Lord will be saved

Who did Jesus die for?

_____

_____

_____

He died for everyone! Just like all have sinned, all can be forgiven.

Some people think that being a good person and doing good things will help them get to Heaven. You should do everything you can to be a good person like helping others and listening to your parents and teachers. But, it is important to know that being a good person is not what allows you to go to Heaven.

All we have to do is call on Him, believe in Him, ask to be forgiven, and He will forgive us. When you receive God's forgiveness, you receive His free gift of salvation.

You may hear some people use the word repent along with forgiveness. When you repent, you express remorse (or say sorry) for your sin. Repentance is more than just being sorry, though. When you repent and ask God to forgive you, you are turning away from your sin and turning toward God.

Romans 10:9-13

If you declare with your mouth, "Jesus is Lord," and believe in your heart that God raised him from the dead, you will be saved. For it is with your heart that you believe and are justified, and it is with your mouth that you profess your faith and are saved. As Scripture says, "Anyone who believes in him will never be put to shame." For there is no difference between Jew and Gentile—the same Lord is Lord of all and richly blesses all who call on him, for, "Everyone who calls on the name of the Lord will be saved."

How do you receive God's free gift of salvation?

_____

_____

_____

_____

Have you asked God to forgive you?

_____

_____

_____

HIS LIFE SAVED MY LIFE ➤ROMANS 5:8

If you have not yet asked God to forgive you, there are no magic words or secret formula. Basically, you just have to ask. You can use your own words or you can pray a prayer like this:

Dear God,

Thank you for sending Jesus to die on the cross. I believe Jesus was the ultimate sacrifice to cover the cost of my sin. I ask you now to forgive me of all my sin, for all the bad things I have done. Help me stop doing things that are wrong and help me start doing the things You want me to do.

Thank you for your gift of salvation. Thank you for forgiving me and making a way for me to spend forever with you. Help me live the rest of my life serving you.

Amen

If you said that prayer (or a similar prayer), the angels in heaven are rejoicing because you are now forgiven and will spend forever in heaven with God! Be sure to tell the important people in your life about your decision (parents, grandparents, pastor, teacher, friends.) Let me know too! Send me an email: ron@pastorronbrooks.com

What now

If you asked God to forgive you and you accepted his gift of salvation, you may be wondering what comes next.

The Bible says you are now a new creation. The old ways are gone. That means your life is now different.

Read 2 Corinthians 5:17

Based on everything you have studied so far, what do you think it means to be "in Christ?"

_____

_____

_____

Have you ever seen a caterpillar spin a cocoon? It normally finds a leaf or a branch and spins a silk cocoon around itself. Do you know why? It does that in order to transform into a beautiful butterfly. That is similar to what the bible says happens to us when we accept God's gift of salvation. We transform into a new creation, just like the butterfly.

Read Psalm 119:105

 What is the word?

_____

_____

_____

How can you hide God's word in your heart?

_____

_____

Now read Matthew 4:1-11

How did Jesus respond when the devil tempted him?

_____

_____

_____

_____

What can you do differently next time you are tempted to do something wrong?

_____

_____

_____

_____

_____

How will knowing the Bible help you stay away from sin?

_____

_____

_____

_____

_____

The devil did all he could to trick Jesus, but every time Jesus used the Bible to fight against the temptation. The devil even tried to use Bible verses himself, but he twisted the words. Jesus knew better and resisted the temptation, and quoted Bible verses back. Finally, the devil knew he would not succeed, so he left.

There will be times that you are tempted. Having Bible verses memorized, or hidden in your heart, will help you overcome temptation.

Submit yourselves, then, to God. Resist the devil, and he will flee from you. James 4:7

How can you resist the devil when he is tempting you?

_____

_____

_____

_____

_____

_____

Reading and learning your Bible is an important part of your faith journey. But those aren't the only things that will help. Going to church and praying are two other things you should know about.

Read Hebrews 10:24-25

Going to church is one way you can meet together. Can you think of some benefits of meeting together? The verses you just read will tell you a few benefits.

_____

_____

_____

_____

_____

Now read Colossians 3:16

What are some other things that happen when you meet together at church?

_____

_____

_____

_____

_____

The church is a place to learn and grow. When you listen to the teachings at church, it will help you learn more about God. And when you sing songs to God, that is a way to worship. Learning and worshipping are ways you can grow in your faith and find out more about God.

One last thing you can do is pray. Some people think that prayer has to be something official using lots of big words. A very simple way to think about prayer is talking and listening to God.

Read James 1:5, James 5:13-16, Psalm 107:28

What do these verses say about prayer?

_____

_____

_____

_____

_____

According to these verses, when should you pray?

_____

_____

_____

_____

_____

Congratulations! You completed your workbook! Hopefully you have a better understanding of salvation and what Jesus did for you. You now know how to grow in your faith. Keep this workbook with you for those times you may have questions. You can refer back to the pages and explanations if you forget. Or, use it to explain to someone else what salvation is!

Now that you are done, if you still have questions about God, salvation, or faith, you can ask a trusted adult-your parents, a teacher, or a pastor. You can also send me an email if you would like, and I will do my best to answer your questions.

ron@pastorronbrooks.com

I am praying for you!

These are the things I am praying about for you:

- That you would understand and accept God's gift of salvation
- That you would grow in your faith
- That you would do your very best to follow God as long as you live
- Send me an email if there is something specific you would like me to pray for

As you continue growing in your faith, when you think you might be ready to be baptized, be sure to check out "A Kid's Guide to Baptism."

"A Kid's Guide to Baptism" is a workbook written to help you understand what baptism means, and reasons why you should be baptized. Just like this workbook, you will read through scriptures and answer some tough questions as you work through your faith and determine if you are ready to take the next step and be baptized. You will also learn how to prepare a personal testimony as you prepare to make a public declaration of your faith.

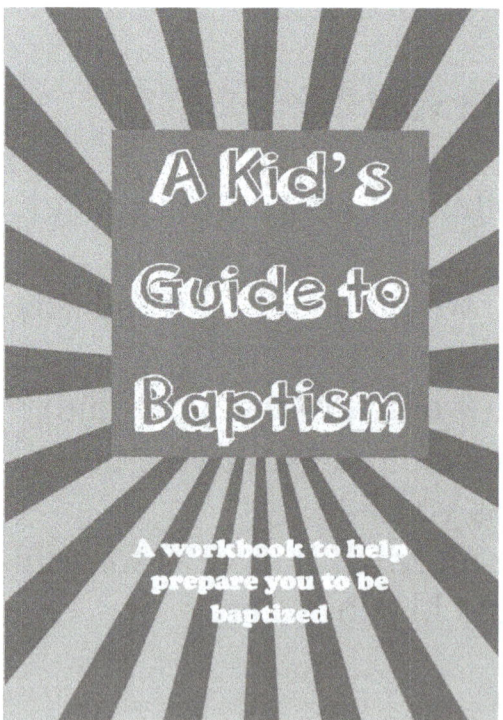

Questions I have

Questions I have

Notes

Notes

Notes

www.ingramcontent.com/pod-product-compliance
Lightning Source LLC
Chambersburg PA
CBHW061721120626
46550CB00003B/1315